HIS GRACE

Is Sufficient

HIS GRACE

Is Sufficient

Jessie Brown

Book design by *River Sanctuary Publishing Graphic Art*
Back cover image courtesy of Soda Bear; *deviantart.com*

ISBN 978-1-935914-38-9

Printed in the United States of America

To order additional copies please visit:
www.riversanctuarypublishing.com

River Sanctuary Publishing
P.O Box 1561
Felton, CA 95018
www.riversanctuarypublishing.com
Dedicated to the awakening of the New Earth

CONTENTS

Chapter I

THE MEDIATOR

Plan

I John 4:14, *And we have seen and do testify that the Father sent the Son to be the Saviour of the world.*

God established a plan for our salvation through the first man, Adam, but Adam didn't remain faithful to the plan. So therefore God had to finally erase the first humans and begin again; making sure that His grace was extended through until eternity. When He, God, re-established the fruitfulness of man, he made sure there was a way for man to return unto Him through a mediator that He could trust to be faithful until the plan for his salvation for mankind was established. This is a very loving Father who took the time to make sure that His people are saved and secured from the bondage and slavery of this wicked world. Man had to be taught how to live for the only true and living God. Therefore it was decided that God would send his word to represent him so that man could receive his grace and mercy, and live for God. Man had been sinful for so long until he had no way back unto the Father. So God gave man a bridge back unto him by sending him a redeemer. A redeemer that could buy back man's freedom for one price; and that was to die. For the man Adam brought sin into the world and one man was to deliver man, and the cost was so great that God gave us glory and sent his one and only Son to earth to redeem man.

*****

For scripture tells us,

> **Romans 5:15,** *"But not as the offense so also is the free gift. For if though the offence of one many be dead, much more the grace of God and the gift by grace which is by one man, Jesus Christ, hath abounded to many. ¹⁶And not as it was be one that sinned so is the gift; for the judgment was by one to condemnation. But the free gift is of many offenses unto justification. ¹⁷For if by one man's offense death reigned by one; much more they which receive abundance of grace and of the gift of righteousness shall reign in life by the Jesus Christ."*

Paul says, look God gave you a way out. Man could not and will not be able to destroy God's plan, but when God establishes a way, nothing can block or turn it away. Oh Glory to God. God is on the throne and we have the victory to live for and through Jesus Christ, glorifying him to his Father. Jesus paid the price to be our mediator for life; so look up and live through Jesus Christ. This is the plan for us to receive Jesus Christ as the head of our lives; become one totally with him, submitting unto his will and way through the living Holy Spirit.

*****

I Timothy 2:5, *"For there is one God, and one mediator between God and men, The Man, Christ Jesus."*

Scripture declares that there was only one mediator and there is only one God by whom he established the perfect plan for salvation.

*****

Hebrews 8:6, *"But now hath he obtained a more excellent ministry, by how much also he is the mediator of a better covenant, was established upon better promises."*

Hebrews 9:15, *"And for this cause he is the mediator of the New Testament, that by means of death, for the redemption of the transgressions that were under the first testament, they which are called might receive the promise of eternal inheritance."*

Hebrews 12:24, *"And to Jesus the mediator of the new covenant, and to the blood of sprinkling that speaketh better things than that of Abel."*

Adam had his chance to keep the plan alive and failed, and it was prophesied down through generation after generation that a Saviour would come to deliver man from himself. God knew that the only way he could deliver man was to send a mediator who was upright, forsake the sinfulness of the flesh and mortify the deeds of the body. And be in control as he taught the people how to love, serve and keep one another, to know that God loved his people and would provide for them, protect them, shield them from hurt, harm and danger. Therefore came Jesus Christ to save man from himself.

*****

I John 4:15, *"Whosoever shall confess that Jesus is the Son of God, God dwelleth in him and he in God."*

So now we know that the plan is established and the covenant made; we have a way out of sin into eternity. Praise God. Thank You Jesus. We also must remember that the plan held defeat for the fall of sin through Jesus Christ, our mediator.

CHAPTER II

THE PURPOSE

The Father

Ephesians 3:11, *"According to the eternal purpose which he purposed in Christ Jesus our Lord."*

THE WORD PURPOSE gives us direction for a plan or idea that will gain benefit for a goal that we have set for our lives. In the same manner, God has derived a plan for salvation from the very beginning of time, for he has purpose that we, the people, listen to his instruction in the Bible; for he has led and given instruction from the beginning of time.

*****

Proverbs 20:18, *"Every purpose is established by counsel: and with good advice make war."*

What is God saying to his people? What better source for counsel can a person go to for instruction, or help for any problem or circumstance that should arise during the course of this great plan God has established. He (God) knows every device or trick of the devil and we know that he is a defeated foe; so when he comes at us with a deception, the discernment of the Spirit through God will give you a way out. Answer me one question, who knows the purpose better than God? He is the master builder for salvation to be gained in this great plan and purpose.

We know that when we don't follow the plan and purpose for God's will, that he can be an awesome and jealous God.

*****

Jeremiah 51:29, "...and the Land shall tremble and sorrow for every purpose shall be performed against Babylon, to make the land of Babylon a desolation without an inhabitant."

We know that God can do exactly what his word tells us he can do. One thing I advise you is that you do not make God chastise you, for you will regret it. I know that he chastens those he loves; but he once told me as I wrote that when he (God) pulls away from our sins, it begins to feel like winter. Oh how I love to repent and obey our God's instructions, for **Psalms 32:7-9** says,

"Thou art my hiding place, thou shalt preserve me from trouble; thou shalt compass me about with songs of deliverance. Selah (peace). 8I will instruct thee and teach thee in the way which thou shalt go. I will guide thee with mine eye. 9...Be ye not as the horse, or as the mule, which have no understanding."

God says listen to my instruction for I established the plan and I know in which direction to lead you. I love you and care for what happens to you. Follow the plan and purpose, as I have given it to you, lest you fall into dire situation. When you do, I will be there to help you.

*****

Acts 11:23, *"Who, when he come and had seen the grace of God, was glad, and exhorted them all, that with purpose of heart they would cleave unto the Lord."*

God said write the laws of my plan upon your hearts and believe in his leadership. Listen to the prophets that he (God) places in the church to lead you out of bondage. God's plan is the only way to establish righteousness to eternity for heaven. He gave us Jesus who was able to become the lamb for us to live; for his death brought us freedom to walk and live for God through Jesus Christ. For Jesus said that he would help us to obtain salvation by obeying the doctrine that he gave us to follow in his footsteps; **Jeremiah 10:23**, *"…for it is not in man that walketh to direct his steps."*

*****

Romans 8:28, *"And we know that all things work together for good to them that love God, to them who are the called according to his purpose."*

Every believer that has received Christ in their life has the responsibility to obey the written word of God. Because when we are going through trials and tribulations, he will bring you through, for he (God) will carry you through the darkest moment of your trial. Your connection through Jesus has paved a way for you and widened your steps, so that you don't fall by the wayside. God's purpose continuously allows us to gain eternal life through his son Jesus Christ.

*****

II Timothy 1:9, *"Who hath saved us, and called us with a Holy calling, not to our works, but according to his own purpose and grace, which was given us in Christ Jesus before the world began."*

Listen, God says that your work cannot and will not get you in, but he has saved you for his own purpose and through Jesus Christ. We must learn to obey, trust, love and follow in Jesus' footsteps, so that we can run this race. For God desires for us to know him better and gain an eternal relationship with him through his only beloved son, Jesus Christ. Only through him and by him will you be able to gain this plan and purpose.

*****

Ephesians 3:11-12, *"According to the eternal purpose which he purposed in Christ Jesus our Lord. [12]In whom we have boldness and access with confidence by the faith of him."*

It cannot be put any clearer that this. Your faith will unlock many doors in this plan that God has for your purpose to please and grow spiritually in his Spirit. We already know that all things work together for our good; so don't allow sin (the devil) to deceive you and make you doubt that you are able to live the purpose that God has for you.

*****

I John 3:8, *"He that committeth sin is of the devil; for the devil sinneth from the beginning."*

For this purpose the son of God was manifested, that he might destroy the works of the devil. Hold on now, we are coming to the end of this chapter. He (God) said that man (Adam) had a chance to prove himself to me. God gave him the entire earth to rule, but what happened? He (Adam) allowed sin to penetrate. The devil thought he could defeat God's plan for salvation, but he was already a defeated foe. So God said no more will he, the devil, be able to stop man and make me destroy the earth completely. I will send my son, the precious Lamb of God, Jesus Christ, who defeated Satan's tactics upon us, so that by faith and trust in his word we would be able to repent and draw closer in our relationship with God for all eternity. Pursuing the purpose for our lives through Jesus, being led by the Living Holy Spirit; walking by faith and not by sight. May God continuously bless us. Feeling it in the Spirit before receiving it and believing that it will come to pass.

CHAPTER III

THE CRISIS

Trials, Tests, Tribulations

Psalms 9:9, *"The Lord also will be a refuge for the oppressed, a refuge in times of trouble."*

WHEN TROUBLE ARISES in our life, we would like nothing better than to run and hide from these things of pain and depression. But we know as Job, a man tried and come out as pure as gold, that we must go through the fire and be tested for strength to hold on to God's unchanging hand, allowing him the benefit of proving His word to us.

*****

Psalms 27:5, *"For in the time of trouble he shall hide me in his pavilion; in the secret of his tabernacle shall he hide me: he shall set me upon a rock."*

We don't have to worry about fighting this battle, for God has already made provisions for us; he has opened up his temple unto us. He has provided shelter in the time of a storm, he will lead and guide us out of the face of danger, he will make your enemy your footstool; all we have to do is call on him and he will answer.

*****

Psalms 37:9, *"For evildoers shall be cut off; but those that wait upon the Lord, they shall inherit the earth."*

He says, don't buckle under the weight and be strong in the Lord. Be content, praise me for what you have, and be patient for what you need; for I will never leave you nor forsake you; hope in those things that are eternal and wait upon me; for I shall and will supply your every need.

*****

Psalms 46:1, *"God is our refuge and strength, a very present help in trouble."*

The word is very encouraging. He says when you are weak, I am strong, lean on me, depend on me, I will give you shelter in your troubles. I have already covered you with the blood of my son. He has redeemed you from your sins, therefore I am opened unto your cries. I will be a refuge for you, for I am kindness, love and understanding. I am your father, I am God.

*****

Psalms 91:15, *"He shall call upon me; and I will answer him: I will be with him in trouble: I will deliver him, and honor him."*

Call upon him, he is waiting for you to focus your attention on him, forsaking the tactics of the devil, for you are not able to defeat him, but through Jesus Christ you have a weapon of warfare, for he can do exceedingly abundantly above all that we can ask, can think or do; Jesus is the way out.

*****

Proverbs 12:13, *"The wicked is snared by the transgression of his lips: but the just shall come out of trouble."*

See you have been redeemed and don't have to fight this battle physically, but spiritually, by faith through Jesus Christ, for we are saved and know that we live in this world, but are not of it: for we must seek and worship him in spirit and truth.

*****

II Corinthians 4:8, *"We are troubled on every side: yet not distressed; we are perplexed but not in despair."*

Paul says rejoice, for the enemy cannot slay you because we will never be taken down, because we have a powerful weapon, Jesus. So all we have to do is stand, pray and rest in Jesus, while he makes our enemies our footstool.

*****

Hebrews 12:1-3, *"Wherefore seeing we also are compassed about with so great a cloud of witnesses, let us lay aside every weight and the sin which doth so easily beset us, and let us run with patience the race that is set before us. ²Looking unto Jesus the author and finisher of our faith; who for the joy that was set before him endured the cross, despising the shame, and is* *set down at the right hand of the throne of God. ³For consider him that endured such contradiction of sinners against himself, lest ye be wearied and faint in your minds?"*

Paul says you must bear your cross, enduring the affliction, demonic attacks, test, trials and tribulations but know that you don't have to bear it alone, for by faith in our Lord and Saviour, Jesus Christ. The battle was fought and the victory was won; on all who would believe that he (Jesus) died and his father raised him (Jesus) from the dead shall be saved, you gain salvation, you have the protection of the armour, for you wrestle against principalities, powers and rulers of this darkened world. As soldier of this vast army, if you are not girded up, then you need to put on the whole armour of God: The Helmet of Salvation, The Shield of Faith, The Breast Plate of Righteousness, Loins Girded about with Truth, Feet shod in the preparation of the Gospel of Peace, and The Sword of the Spirit, which is the Word of God. In other words, you need to be saved, walking in Jesus, through the spirit of God, and studying the Word of God, so that you may get an understanding of how to fight through Jesus Christ our Lord and Saviour. He will hide you and protect, shield and guide you through all earthly dangers.

CHAPTER IV

THE TRUST

In God

Proverbs 3:5, 6, *"Trust in the Lord with all thine heart; and lean not unto thine own understanding. In all thy ways acknowledge him, an he shall direct thy path."*

W E KNOW THAT our success on this journey depends on whether we trust in the Lord with all of our hearts and lean not to our own understanding; but there are times when our motives do not allow for trust from one that loves us more than we or anyone else can possibly love us. I am thinking maybe, if we understand the precepts or definition of the word "trust" then maybe we can gear up our motives to please our father and God more. Let's look at the word trust: rely, depend, to be assured, to be able to get a definite answer, to know that it will work to your good. Well believe this, the God that said trust in me with all your heart, meant just that; because only he knows the plan and the purpose for your being. For he told Jeremiah, I knew you before you were born, I ordain your walk and because of my love that I give you authority and a free gift of salvation. I will bring in one better than all; he sent Jesus to bridge the gap between man and God, so what better source than to trust in God almighty. Hallelujah, Thank You Jesus!

*****

Psalms 4:5, *"Offer the sacrifices of righteousness and put your trust in the Lord."*

He says, don't continue to walk in your ways but abandon them, and I will show you a better way. Jesus has redeemed and set you free, therefore you have a voice. Make the correct choice and you will be able to live free of this world's sins for I will help stabilize you spiritually, if you let me. When trouble arises, call on me and await my answer for I am Jehovah-Jireh and I will provide for you. I will allow my spirit to keep you holy and living righteous in my eyesight, now don't be as the mule, and buck my authority. Jesus died and paid the cost for you to live in him; for Paul says to trust in him, for him to live is Christ and to die is gain. That is total trust; can you climb that ladder of success in Christ?

*****

Psalms 40:3, 4, *"And he hath put a new song in my mouth, even praise unto our God: many shall see it, and fear, and shall trust in the Lord ⁴Blessed is the man that maketh the Lord his trust and respecteth not the proud nor such as turn aside to lies."*

God says keep focused on me, for I will give you a new song to sing while I make your enemy your footstool. I am your provider in the time of a storm, I am your shelter and your keeper from all evil. Paul said that we are more than conquerors in

Christ Jesus. Jesus will lead you through the comforter (the Living Holy Spirit) for he knows the mysteries of the plan and purpose for your life through Jesus and God. Jesus is praying in intercessory prayer for you, hoping that you will remember to trust in the almighty God for your every need.

*****

Psalms 5:11, *"But let all those that put their trust in thee rejoice: let them ever shout for joy, because thou defendest them: let them that also love thy name be joyful in thee."*

He says you know who I am, you have a relationship with me. You are going through the process of growing within me spiritually, so don't quit on me now. Don't rely on man who cannot deliver you with joy, peace and understanding. Paul says count it all joy when you come upon diverse situations, for your joy and praise can deliver you, for when the enemy comes in like a flood, the spirit of the Lord will lift up a standard against him. He will protect you and shield you. Just stay focused on Jesus and watch God move on your behalf. Thank you Jesus.

*****

Psalms 56:11, *"In God have I put my trust: I will not be afraid what man can do unto me."*

Hold on saints, for if you fear, then God cannot move. God's timing is not like ours, for a thousand years is like one day, but if you just continue to hold on when the rain starts and not fear, then God will come through for you. When fear begins remember God did not give you a spirit of fear but of power, and love, and a sound mind, and also that God has total control over all things in this universe.

*****

Proverbs 16:20, *"He that handleth a matter wisely shall find good: and whosoever trusteth in the Lord, happy is he."*

Thank God for his word for it is truly instruction for the believer to engage and walk this walk in boldness. You can be sure of a wise decision when you consult the Lord's guidance in our lives, for he (God) will never deceive or trick us, for these are the devices of the enemy. God cannot lie; his word is truth, quick and powerful. It can pierce a lie and shred it to pieces. Believe God's word and be happy, healthy and safe. When you become happy, don't become proud and boisterous, because you have nothing to boast about. The Lord is your shepherd and your deliverer.

*****

Proverbs 28:25, *"He that is of a proud heart stirreth up strife, but he that putteth his trust in the Lord shall be made fat."*

As long as you remember that God delivered you and walk in humbleness, love, peace, joy, tolerance; patience, fellowship with others, putting the Lord first in your life, and not overlooking others, but everything is me, me, me and I, I, I. Then you will not prosper in the joy of the Lord.

*****

Let us look at **Proverbs 29:25,**

"The fear of man bringeth a snare, but whoso putteth his trust in the Lord shall be safe."

These instructions from God have been instrumental in shedding light on so many things that tend to snare us as we walk daily in the light of Jesus, for sometimes when we know the way, we tend to slip a little. But the thing we do know for sure is to repent and know we have a loving, caring father that looks out for us, cares, protecting and shielding us from all hurt and harm. All he asks is that we learn to share with one another, don't brow beat, dodge or shun each other, for he uses us to care for one another's needs. As we depend, rely and love him, he will bless us in strength, joy, spiritual growth, humbleness, tolerance, patience, brotherly love, guidance, peace, honesty and hindsight to keep us trusting in God through Jesus Christ and kept by his Holy Spirit. Trust in the Lord and be blessed for he shall make your enemy your footstool. Hallelujah, Thank You Jesus.

The key to this trust is faith, for with faith, you can gain entry into the spiritual realm of God. You can grow through faith for it unlocks the door to Jesus' heart. Faith can move mountains, can prevent a storm arising, begin to pray and praise God for the victory. Stand on his promises for God cannot lie. Faith opens up the door to trust; you will not be able to trust if you don't have faith.

BELIEVE in God and RECEIVE. Thank You Jesus, bless your holy name.

Chapter V

THE G-R-A-C-E

Psalms 84:11, *"For the Lord is a sun and shield; the Lord will give grace and glory: no good thing will he withhold from them that walk upright."*

GOD'S LOVE IS indescribable, it's elegance is so pure and moving that you can't see it, nor can you touch it. But it wraps you in a coat of warmth that can keep you strong in any situation in your life. God's love paved the way for us to gain eternal life by looking beyond man's sins and gives humankind an escape through the death of his one and only son, Jesus; precious lamb of life. Now tell me how can you describe a love like that, one that is unconditional? Well, with the help of the living Holy Spirit, I will try to expound on the GRACE of God, which is his unmerited favor for man in sin.

The beauty of God's love came through Jesus who was born of a woman whom God had found virtuous to carry his seed for nine months. Jesus was born of woman to carry the sins of man to the cross. He was 100% man and 100% GOD. Therefore, God had complete control over his precious and dear son. Jesus became a bridge for mankind to God for then God could see the goodness of man through Jesus who had made a covenant with man through the cross. By God manifesting his love through Jesus, then Jesus found favor and shone brightly for God; showing man how to walk and live in the flesh. So they could gain God's unmerited love, which is now a free gift to all nations and people, for God loves a sinner and is always merciful unto us all. Believe that the Superior God of this great universe loves us all unconditionally.

*****

John 1:16, 17, "And his fullness have all we received, and grace for grace. 17For the law was given by Moses, but grace and truth came by Jesus Christ."

Know that you could not receive the unmerited favor of God until his son, Jesus, came and bridged the gap. Now that we have the bridge, we must learn to take advantage of the freedom that can only be found through and in Jesus Christ. There is no other hope for man, woman or child, if you don't gain eternal life through Jesus. There is definitely no other way to gain his grace. This grace is the freely given unmerited love of God; he cares about you and everything that you do. Once we obtain this gift, then we must learn how to allow Jesus through His spirit to lead and keep us in this grace. I must say that obtaining and keeping favor in God's eyesight through Jesus is a growing process. Thank You Jesus. Hallelujah.

*****

Romans 11:5, *"Even so then at this present time also there is a remnant according to the election of grace. Jesus is saying even though he bridged the gap, only a small portion will remain."*

So therefore it is very important that we learn to live for God, and not ourselves because we have nothing to boast about here on this earth. But we have a great testimony through the work and doctrine of Jesus Christ. Learn all about his teachings, for he only taught for a few years before he gave his life for all mankind. He had a very interesting, compassionate, loving walk. He had all power and authority over devices and to cure diseases. He made it easy for us to grasp hold and understand the needs that exist in our lives and others; for his teaching was for everyone to receive the free gift of an unmerited love.

*****

II Timothy 1:9, 10, *"Who hath saved us, and called us, with an holy call, not according to our works, but according to his own purpose and grace, which was given us in Christ Jesus before the world began. ¹⁰But is now made manifest by the appearing of our Saviour Jesus Christ, who hath abolished death, and hath brought life and immortality to light through the gospel."*

Hallelujah! He said now that I have gone to the cross, been executed, died and shed my blood for the remission of sins in this world. You can go forth and allow me to use your bodies as vessels in spreading the gospel so that many more can gain life through me. I want people to feel this unconditional love I have. So let your little light shine for me. The more that the word is expounded, reproved and reproofed, the more the gift will be shared.

*****

I Peter 5:5, *"Likewise ye younger, submit yourselves unto the elder. Yea, all of you be subject one to another, and be clothed with humility: for God resisteth the proud, and giveth grace to the humble."*

Jesus instructs us to teach the young and show them how to be humble and have respect for the elders (i.e. king and queenagers). These instructions are for everyone, for we must help all receive salvation for it is the free gift of God's unmerited grace. Man cannot grant this unto you, but it can be earned by giving your life to Jesus Christ in exchange for eternal life. You cannot work and gain it, but you must make a commitment through living for Christ and believe that you can gain a personal relationship with God.

*****

Acts 15:11, *"But we believed that through the grace of the Lord Jesus Christ we shall be saved, even as they."*

Once we accept Jesus Christ into our lives, then we must strive to live as holy as we possibly can for this is a divine relationship that we are acquiring. We must endeavor to have the mind of Christ in order for God's influence through the living Holy Spirit to step in and help to keep us clean. For once we are accepted by Christ, then we are to learn how to grow according to the word. The Bible clearly gives us instructions for growth, it tells parents to raise their children up in the admonition of the Lord; tells the children to obey their parents for this is right in the eyesight of the Lord; instructs us as brothers and sisters in Christ that we must not continue to be selfish in watching over what is ours, but must look to the other person and give help as needed. But do we do this? The instructions of Jesus are very clear and unless we can obey them all in love, peace, joy, temperance, longsuffering, brotherly love, faith, honesty, goodness, gentleness and meekness. Unless you have the fruits of the spirit, how can you carry your cross? Repent, for God loves a repentant heart for then he can use you to do his will and not your will.

*****

Romans 3:24, 25, *"Being justified freely by his grace through the redemption that is in Christ Jesus. [25]Whom God hath set forth to be a propitiation through faith in his blood, to declare his righteousness for the remission of sins that are past through the forbearance of God."*

Through the scriptures we can see the testimony of Christ in his righteousness in going to the cross, paying the debt that we owed, so that we can glorify him to his father, which is in heaven. God has blessed us to have and gain a personal relationship with him through Jesus Christ. There is no other way that you can gain eternal life except through Jesus Christ. God justified him through his dying, so that the bridging of the gap between him and man could be made. Jesus had to redeem man from himself because he had destroyed himself and every way out for anyone else. So God sent the word and the word became flesh, enabling man to have a way to escape.

*****

Romans 4:4, *"Now to him that worketh, is the reward not reckoned of grace, but of debt."*

What is he saying? In Abraham's day, he was justified by his righteousness but the sins of the world had become so great that God had decided that it was time for a mediator because people could not be trusted to live right for any length of time.

So therefore we have our mediator, Jesus, who came, worked and died so that we might have a chance at eternal life.

*****

Ephesians 2:5, *"Even when we were dead in sin, hath quick-ened us together with Christ."*

By grace ye are saved. There ye have it, through Jesus Christ, our mediator, came salvation to life. He saved and gave life, for Jesus is our source of life and our life line. Once you truly feel the effects of a holy walk with God, you will thirst for more. Your desires will become immense for a closer walk, a holier walker. You endeavor to be all you can, you confess your weaknesses, your inability to maintain a healthy relationship with him. But oh, allow Jesus to work it out for you and you will be able to speak from the mountain tops. Pray the solution, walk bold and humble, love right, climb the ladder of grace through Jesus' eyesight before his father, God.

*****

II Corinthians 1:12, *"For our rejoicing is this, the testimony of our conscience that in simplicity and Godly sincerity, not with fleshly wisdom, but by the grace of God."*

We have had our conversation in the world and worried about things of the world. Let us not continue thinking worldly, but rejoice that now we can handle these things through Jesus Christ, who can help us rejoice when we have bad times and good times. But we must be sincere in our endeavors for the Lord, giving our utmost in every respect, for God wants us to be real at all times. For when we walk and strive to be an exact example of Christ, then the better the effect we will have on the lost souls of this world.

*****

I Peter 4:10, *"As every man hath received the gift, even so minister the same one to another, as good stewards a/the manifold grace a/God."*

God said ask me for wisdom, knowledge and understanding. I will give it liberally; you must strive to be a good steward in the ministry, so that the blessings of God can be multiplied. There are many who need the help of the saints and believers so that they can participate in the work of the kingdom. Be led by the Holy Spirit, have faith and trust in God for your help and stability. He loves you and wants to instruct you, teach you the way to go and guide you with his eye.

*****

Titus 2:11-15, *"For the grace of God that bringeth salvation hath appeared to all men. ¹²Teaching us that denying ungodliness and worldly lusts, we should live soberly, righteously and Godly, in this present world; ¹³Looking for that blessed hope, and the glorious appearing of the great God and our Saviour Jesus Christ. ¹⁴Who gave himself for us, that he might redeem us from all iniquity, and purity unto himself a peculiar people zealous of good works. ¹⁵These things speak and exhort, and rebuke with all authority. Let no man despise."*

This plan was established by God, and it cannot work any other way except through and by Jesus Christ. Go into the highways and byways being good stewards of God's written instructions, harvesting the crop that is ripe for the picking, being effective and giving God the glory through his son, Jesus Christ, bearing the fruits of the spirit. For we live in this world and are not of it, desiring to bear our crosses in this vast army of the Lord. God loves you, Jesus loves you, the living Holy Spirit loves you, and so do I. May God richly bless and strengthen you to do His work. Good Grace was given unto us through Jesus Christ.

G = God's

R = Relationship

A = At

C = Christ's

E = Expense

G-R-A-C-E

www.ingramcontent.com/pod-product-compliance
Lightning Source LLC
Chambersburg PA
CBHW021349090426
42742CB00008B/798